Dr. Karlene Fray

Contact the Author:
Karlenetwo@yahoo.com

TABLE OF CONTENTS

INTRODUCTION

I am profoundly grateful to God for this download and humbled to share this revelation with you. I am so excited to unpack this revelation and to take this journey with you as we discover God's plans for singles.

Living as a single person is not a disadvantage, but a God-given assignment to His chosen people. How we manage our singleness and the recognition of our purpose, will change the trajectory of our lives.

It's time to level up and power up!

Singles are not incomplete individuals, waiting on their better halves, or obsessed with sex, but they are God's master creation, made in His image, and are empowered to dominate and increase.

Shift your mind and let's go!

S – **Stand Tall**

T – **Tower over your Circumstances**

A **Activate your God-given Power**

R – **Rule in your Realm**

SINGLENESS IS NOT JUST A STATUS; IT IS AN ASSIGNMENT.

Regardless of your circumstances, whether you have been separated, divorced, widowed, or never been married, you are at an exciting time of your life. You are chosen by God and He is counting on you to fulfill your purpose and enjoy life.

According to - 1 Corinthians 7:34; "The unmarried woman/man careth for the things of the Lord, that she/he may be holy, both in body, and in spirit."

Singleness is an assignment: it is a course, task, and designation that God bestows on those who are unmarried. The power of obedience is a deadly weapon against the enemy. As a holy, set apart vessel, God is counting on singles to rise up in their power, authority and shine for Jesus.

Singles are called to focus on the ministry of God and to utilize their gifts and talents to benefit the kingdom. They are created to maximize every God-given opportunity and to be successful. Individually, they are graced for the scope of their unique assignment and endowed with the provisions to execute it.

According to Webster's dictionary, the word "**assignment**" is defined as an act of assigning something such as a task; a position, post, or office to which one is assigned a specified task, or amount of work given or undertaken.

Therefore, singles are set in position to execute the task that God has specifically given to them.

As a Single person:

- You are a powerful, single-minded warrior for God. • You are God's consecrated portion.

- You are growing into your assignment.

- You are discovering yourself and your God-given gifts and talents.

- You are allowing yourself to mature, heal, and develop.

- You are made in the image of God.

- You are made 100% complete.

- You are building and establishing your foundation.

- You are experiencing life and building a legacy.

- You are having fun and enjoying life.

Your assignment is conditional on God giving you a spouse, if that is your desire. It is not a life sentence, but a season that God allows singles to be undistracted, unattached, and a gift to others.

Enjoy your gift of singleness and see it as:

- A place of prayer, power, and purity.

- Time to grow in your relationship with God.
- You are chosen by God for such an assignment.
- You are endowed by God with the grace for your singleness.
- God loves you and there is a change in time and season in the assignment.
- Singleness means you can purposefully live your life to the dictates of heaven.
- You are a "good thing" worth finding.
- You are valuable and know your worth.

In the book of Genesis, God created Adam as a single person before he got married to Eve. Adam was created in the image of God to dominate and rule in the earth realm.

He was intelligent and success was already embedded in his DNA. He was equipped to carry out his purpose and fulfill his assignment. Adam was made completely whole, not half or 50% of a person waiting for Eve to complete him.

It is unclear how long Adam was single, but we are certain that it was God's design and it pleased Him. It is pleasing to God when singles walk in their divine destiny, purpose, and bring glory to His name.

Gen 2: 7 (KJV) says, "And the Lord God formed man of the dust of the ground and breathed into his nostrils the breath of life, and man became a living soul."

We are created as triune being consisting of three parts - body, soul, and spirit:

Spirit: God-conscious part of man - spirit man

Soul: Self-conscious part of man- will, mind and emotion

Body: World-conscious part of man – physical man/body

Living single does NOT mean:

- You are incomplete and inferior.
- You are an unsuccessful person until marriage.
- You are sad and lonely.
- You are a status identification.
- You are to be ashamed of your life.
- You are one half of a person waiting to find your other half.
- You are obsessed with finding a spouse.
- Your life is on hold until you are married.

- You are (fill in the blank).

____

____

Rather, your assignment requires you to:

- Be pure in mind, body, and soul.
- Be single-minded and mentally stable.
- Submit to the leadership of the Holy Spirit.
- Build-up yourself in the word of God.
- Be totally surrendered to God.
- Grow and mature.
- Enjoy the assignment and the journey
- Discover who you are.
- Heal from any hurt, pain, negativity, and dysfunctions.
- Maximize your potential.

Powerful Single People in the Bible:

- **Daniel** – A prophet of God who was skilled in understanding and interpretation of dreams. He received apocalyptic dreams/visions from God. He was full of faith, wisdom, and had superior intelligence. Daniel was a government official under four Babylonian kings. He was thrown in the lion's den and came out unharmed because God protected him. He was the only one, who was able to reveal and interpret the dream of King Nebuchadnezzar.

- **Three Hebrew Boys** - Shadrach, Meshach, and Abednego (Hananiah, Mishael, and Azariah) were brought from Israel to Babylon. They possessed exceptional intelligence, wisdom, and worked as government officials in the Babylonian courts. They have exceptional faith in God and boldness. They refused to worship the golden image of King Nebuchadnezzar and as a result were thrown in the fire. Jesus showed up in the fire with them and they were unharmed. King Nebuchadnezzar was astonished and commanded their release. The King promoted them and ordered people everywhere to the honor the God of Shadrach, Meshach, and Abednego.

- **Jeremiah –** A prophet of God called from his mother's womb. He was an author and a reformer. He was fearless and faithful to God. Although the message was hard to proclaim, he did not compromise but stood tall with integrity and trusted God. He was not popular; however, he was faithful and proclaimed God's message to Israel.

- **Nehemiah –** served in the Persian royal court as cupbearer to King Artaxerxes. He secured funds and organized the rebuilding of the walls of Jerusalem. Later, he was named the Governor of Judah. Nehemiah was strategic and focused on the completion of the wall despite the opposition. He brought the people of God from captivity and led them back to God.

- **John the Baptist –** was the son of Zachariah the High Priest, a great Evangelist, and the forerunner of Jesus. He dedicated his life telling the people "to repent" and proclaimed the coming of the messiah Jesus Christ.

- **Anna –** She chose to remain a widow for the rest of her life. She was a prophetess who devoted her life to fasting, praying, and ministering in the temple. She prayed for and witnessed the manifestation of the coming of Jesus and the redemption of Israel.

- **Martha, Mary, and Lazarus –** They are remarkably close friends of Jesus. Jesus stayed at their home when he visited their town. He raised Lazarus from the dead.

- **You -** Fill in your name and accomplishments:

____

____

____

____

____

____

____

____

____

THE ASSIGNMENT IS BIGGER THAN YOU THINK!

Let us live our lives so that others will be able to honor the God that we serve. The assignment is great, and I am challenging you to embrace it with faith and go for it. Cancel the voice of fear and step out in boldness. One step at a time, just keep walking, and sooner or later, you will begin to take giant steps. God is counting on you; heaven is cheering you on, so take the leap of faith.

Go after the assignment, seek the things of God and He will guide and make the provision for the journey. Quit worrying about when your Boaz or Eve will come but go after your dreams and set yourself in place for the blessings.

Honor the Assignment!

Honor the assignment that God has given you and make full proof of your ministry. Remain submitted and dedicated to the Lord. Let the mind of Christ be formed in you, also, and be attentive to the voice of God. God is counting on you, and others are counting on you to complete your assignment.

2 Timothy 4:5 (AMP) says, "But as for you, be clearheaded in every situation [stay calm and cool and steady], endure every hardship [without flinching], do the work of an evangelist, fulfill [the duties of] your ministry."

What is the assignment?

I am glad you asked. The assignment is building a legacy, develop economies, lay the foundation for the next generation, multiply, and increase. The success of your assignment is already guaranteed and backed by heaven. There is no failure in God, if we put our faith in Him and walk in obedience.

Let us unpack the reality of the assignment:

- **Legacy:** Build a spiritual and natural legacy for the next generation to inherit. Use your experiences, struggles, and victories to empower others, especially the younger generation. Do not merely pass through the earth but be intentional, impactful and trailblaze the path for others. Leave a mark in the realm of spirit and in the earth that will shift your family, church, community, country, generation, and the nations.

  You may ask how can I accomplish this? It is done through prayer which shifts and changes everything. Start by praying for your family and, break generational curses to release generational blessing. As you spend time in prayer, and reading the word, the Holy Spirit, our master teacher will guide you in all things.

- **Add Value:** Do not be a consumer only but be an investor. Invest in yourself to make a deposit in the lives of others. Make things, situations, and people better. Do not spend your time criticizing and tearing down but build up and reconcile. Invest and mentor others. Be realistic and have fun along the journey.

- **Develop Economies:** Handle your affairs in excellence and be successful as a single person. Manage and administrate your money, property, household, relationships, time, reputation, emotion, and spiritual life. Do not run your single life into spiritual bankruptcy. Be accountable and discerning. Make God approved decisions rather than people-pleasing ones. Grow and make discoveries from your mistakes. Forgive others and yourself. Build your portfolio and create a vision board then work towards accomplishing it. Choose your friends and associations well and watch out for dream killers and discern their motives.

- **Foundation:** Build your foundation on prayer, praise, worship, and the word of God. Make the right steps in becoming debt-free, be financially stable, spiritually empowered, and emotionally whole. Let your foundation be solid and strong. Having a strong foundation will determine the height of your success. A strong foundation will be able to carry the weight of your assignment.

- **Doorkeeper:** Be vigilant, about the things you allow, endorse, post, and agree with. Monitor the doorway of your soul and filter the voices, opinions, ideas, that you permit to enter. Guard your ear and eye gates. Let the Holy Spirit be your teacher, hear and submit to his voice.

- **Multiply:** Be multifaceted and multi-dimensional in your approach. Reproduce only good things and become a better version of yourself. Be the catalyst that motivates and cultivate the best in others. Ask God to download witty ideas and inventions for you and others. Be strategic in your thinking; engage and mobilize with a multinational and global mindset. Think outside of the box and create something that will impact a generation.

- **Increase:** Be actively responsible for your growth and development. Continuously educate, empower, improve your intelligence, and expand your mind. Do not settle, experience the greater things in God and life. Learn and experience new things within the boundary of God's guidance. Never limit the power of God in your life because He is the one that gives the increase. Increase in wisdom, knowledge, understanding, and your spiritual life.

Even though the assignment is great, it does not mean that singles are bound and cannot take time to enjoy life. It is God's desire for us to live our best life and to walk in total victory, happiness, and success. There is freedom in God and here, are some ways to enjoy your single life:

- Embrace your singleness and be happy.
- Learn a new skill or find a Hobby.
- Start a business.
- Stop chasing after people who look successful
- Be spontaneous… lighten up!
- Travel, experience places and different cultures

- Change your job if you are not happy there.
- Read or write books.
- Get a second job and, pay off your debts
- Take time to relax and recharge
- Spend time with family and friends.
- Volunteer your time.
- Help and support your local church.
- Mentor others.
- Fill in the blank

____

____

____

____

____

____

____

____

____

____

____

HERE ARE SOME ENCOURAGING BIBLE VERSES FOR SINGLES:

I will praise thee; *for I am fearfully [and] wonderfully made: marvelous [are] thy works; and [that] my soul knoweth right well. -* *Psalms 139:14*

Have I not commanded you? Be strong and courageous. Do not be afraid; do not be discouraged, for the Lord your God will be with you wherever you go. Joshua 1:9

But seek ye first the kingdom of God, and his righteousness; and all these things shall be added unto you - Matthew 6:33

But ye [are] a chosen generation, a royal priesthood, a holy nation, a peculiar people; that ye should shew forth the praises of him who hath called you out of darkness into his marvelous light - 1 Peter 2:9

The LORD thy God in the midst of thee [is] mighty; he will save, he will rejoice over thee with joy; he will rest in his love, he will joy over thee with singing - Zephaniah 3:17

Behold, what manner of love the Father hath bestowed upon us, that we should be called the sons of God: therefore the world knoweth us not, because it knew him not - 1 John 3:1

..but those who hope in the Lord, renew their strength. They will soar on wings like eagles; they will run and not grow weary, they will walk and not be faint - Isaiah 40:31

So do not fear, for I am with you; do not be dismayed, for I am your God. I will strengthen you and help you; I will uphold you with my righteous right hand - Isaiah 41:10

being confident of this, that he who began a good work in you will carry it on to completion until the day of Christ Jesus - Philippians 1:6

But he said to me, 'My grace is sufficient for you, for my power is made perfect in weakness." Therefore, I will boast all the more gladly about my weaknesses, so that Christ's power may rest on me - 2 Corinthians 12:9

He answered, "Don't be afraid; for those who are with us are more than those who are with them – 2 Kings 6:16

What, then, shall we say in response to these things? If God is for us, who can be against us? - Romans 8:31

A father of the fatherless, and a judge of the widows, is God in his holy habitation. God setteth the solitary in families: he bringeth out those which are bound with chains: but the rebellious dwell in a dry land - Psalm 68:5-6

Casting all your care upon him; for he careth for you. Be sober, be vigilant; because your adversary the devil, as a roaring lion, walketh about, seeking whom he may devour: Whom resist stedfast in the faith, knowing that the same afflictions are accomplished in your brethren that are in the world. But the God of all grace, who hath called us unto his eternal glory by Christ Jesus, after that ye have suffered a while, make you perfect, stablish, strengthen, settle you. To him be glory and dominion for ever and ever. Amen. - 1 Peter 5:7-11

I say therefore to the unmarried and widows, it is good for them if they abide even as I.9 But if they cannot contain, let them marry: for it is better to marry than to burn. - *1 Corinthians 7:8-9*

Be strong and of a good courage: for unto this people shalt thou divide for an inheritance the land, which I swore unto their fathers to give them. Only be thou strong and very courageous, that thou mayest observe to do according to all the law, which Moses my servant commanded thee: turn not from it to the right hand or to the left, that thou mayest prosper withersoever thou goest. This book of the law shall not depart out of thy mouth; but thou shalt meditate therein day and night, that thou mayest observe to do according to all that is written therein: for then thou shalt make thy way prosperous, and then thou shalt have good success...- *Joshua 1:6-8*

And the Lord, he it is that doth go before thee; he will be with thee, he will not fail thee, neither forsake thee: fear not, neither be dismayed --*Deuteronomy 31:8*

When thou passest through the waters, I will be with thee; and through the rivers, they shall not overflow thee: when thou walkest through the fire, thou shalt not be burned; neither shall the flame kindle upon thee. For I am the Lord thy God, the Holy One of Israel, thy Saviour: I gave Egypt for thy ransom, Ethiopia and Seba for thee. Since thou wast precious in my sight, thou hast been honourable, and I have loved thee: therefore, will I give men for thee, and people for thy life. -*Isaiah 43:2-4*

Be careful for nothing; but in everything by prayer and supplication with thanksgiving let your requests be made known unto God. And the peace of God, which passeth all understanding, shall keep your hearts and minds through Christ Jesus - *Philippians 4:6-7*

There hath no temptation taken you but such as is common to man: but God is faithful, who will not suffer you to be tempted above that ye are able; but will with the temptation also make a way to escape, that ye may be able to bear it. - 1 Corinthians 10:13

For the LORD your God [is] he that goeth with you, to fight for you against your enemies, to save you - Deuteronomy 20:4

Seek the LORD and his strength, Seek his face continually - 1 Chronicles 16:11

Then he said unto them, go your way, eat the fat, and drink the sweet, and send portions unto them for whom nothing is prepared: for this day is holy unto our Lord: neither be ye sorry; for the joy of the LORD is your strength. - Nehemiah 8:10

The LORD God is my strength, and he will make my feet like hinds' feet, And he will make me to walk upon mine high places. To the chief singer on my stringed instruments. - Habakkuk 3:19

And thou shalt love the Lord thy God with all thy heart, and with all thy soul, and with all thy mind, and with all thy strength: this is the first commandment. - Mark 12:30

There hath no temptation taken you but such as is common to man: but God [is] faithful, who will not suffer you to be tempted above that ye are able; but will with the temptation also make a way to escape, that ye may be able to bear [it]. - 1 Corinthians 10:13

The LORD is my strength and my shield; My heart trusted in him, and I am helped: Therefore, my heart greatly rejoiceth; And with my song will I praise him. The LORD is their strength, And he is the saving strength of his anointed. - Psalm 28:7-8

It is God that girdeth me with strength, And maketh my way perfect. - Psalm 18:32

Be of good courage, and he shall strengthen your heart, all ye that hope in the LORD. - Psalm 31:24

God is our refuge and strength, A very present help in trouble. - Psalm 46:1

But be not thou far from me, O LORD: O my strength, haste thee to help me. - Psalm 22:19

The LORD is my strength and my shield; My heart trusted in him, and I am helped: Therefore, my heart greatly rejoiceth; And with my song will I praise him. The LORD is their strength, and he is the saving strength of his anointed. - Psalm 28:7-8

PRAYER FOR SINGLES

Father, I honor you for this assignment that you have given me. I submit myself to the process and the task you have ordained for me. Show me the way, renew my mind, and give me the courage to honor this assignment and to maximize my full potential and purpose.

Father, remove all fear, pride, anxiety, doublemindedness, and inner conflict from my life and, add your love. I die to myself and my mind is renewed. I surrender totally to you and I submit myself under your care and government.

Teach me to walk in faith and, to trust you, even when I do not understand. Grant me the wisdom, knowledge, and understanding to work out this assignment. Teach me to be contented with what you have blessed me with. Show me the way, and let your lamp guide my feet and the revelation of your word illuminate my path. Keep my feet from falling and renew my strength like the eagle.

Father, keep me from all distractions and remove the wrong people from my life. Heal me from every hurt, rejection, abandonment, and pain. Free me from the memories of my past and forgive me for my mistakes. I yield myself totally to you today and receive your healing and forgiveness.

I am committed to this assignment, and will carry out this task with integrity, and confidence. I will be steadfast and stand strong regardless of the arrows that comes up against me. I am standing on your promises and your word.

I am confident that when my season changes and this assignment has been completed, you will grant me the desires of my heart as you promised in:

Psalm 37:4 (AMP) that says, Delight yourself in the Lord, And He will give you the desires and petitions of your heart

Psalm 84:11 (KJV) says, For the LORD God is a sun and shield: the LORD will give grace and glory: no good thing will he withhold from them that walk uprightly

- Amen

REFERENCES

The Holy Bible

Merriam-Webster Dictionary

Strong, James. Strong's Expanded Exhaustive Concordance of the Bible. Nashville: Thomas Nelson, 2009

NOTES

www.ingramcontent.com/pod-product-compliance
Lightning Source LLC
LaVergne TN
LVHW010513160826
845677LV00012B/2835

* 9 7 9 8 3 6 1 4 7 0 6 2 4 *